Sojourner Truth

A Photo-Illustrated Biography
by Margo McLoone

Reading Consultant:
Dr. Gail Lowe
Anacostia Museum

Bridgestone Books
an Imprint of Capstone Press

Facts about Sojourner Truth

- Sojourner Truth was a slave for 28 years.
- She first spoke the Dutch language.
- She was never able to read, but she knew parts of the Bible by heart.
- Truth Drive in Battle Creek, Michigan, is named for her.

Bridgestone Books are published by Capstone Press • 818 North Willow Street, Mankato, Minnesota 56001
Copyright © 1997 by Capstone Press • All rights reserved • Printed in the United States of America

Library of Congress Cataloging-in-Publication Data
McLoone, Margo
    Sojourner Truth/by Margo McLoone
    p. cm.--(Read and discover photo-illustrated biographies)
    Includes bibliographical references and index.
    Summary: A brief biography of the abolitionist and women's rights activist who spent
    twenty-eight years of her life as a slave.
    ISBN 1-56065-518-6
    1.Truth, Sojourner, d. 1883--Juvenile literature. 2. Afro-American abolitionists--
Biography--Juvenile literature. 3. Abolitionists--United States--Biography-- Juvenile literature.
4. Social reformers--United States--Biography--Juvenile literature. [1. Truth, Sojourner.
d. 1883. 2. Abolitionists. 3. Reformers. 4. Afro-Americans--Biography. 5. Women--Biography.]
    I. Title. II. Series.
E185.97.T8M385   1997
305.5'67'092
[B]--DC21

                                        96-37382
                                          CIP
                                           AC

Photo credits
Schomberg Center, cover, 4, 18, 20
Bettmann, 6, 8, 10, 14, 16
Unicorn/Flipper, 12

Table of Contents

Famous Speaker

Sojourner Truth wanted equality for all people.
Equality means everyone is treated the same.
She spent much of her life working for freedom
and equality.

Sojourner was a tall, strong woman with a
deep voice. She traveled around the United States
giving speeches.

People listened when she spoke out against
slavery. Slavery means a person is owned by
someone else. People also listened when she spoke
out for women's rights. She believed that women
had the right to vote in elections.

Sojourner was a famous speaker for human
rights. She had a sharp sense of humor. Her speeches
and sayings are still remembered today.

Sojourner wanted all people to be treated equally.

Child of Slavery

In 1799, Sojourner was born in Hurley, New York. Her parents named her Isabella. Their names were Mau-Mau Bett and Baumfree. Many years later, Isabella changed her name to Sojourner Truth. To sojourn means to travel.

Isabella had many brothers and sisters. They were sold to slave traders before she was born. Slave traders bought and sold slaves. Isabella hated slavery because it tore families apart.

When Isabella was nine, she was sold to another slave owner. After that, she was sold two more times and sent to work.

Isabella spent her days picking cotton in the fields. At night, she washed clothes and spun wool. She lived as a slave for 28 years.

Isabella hated slavery because it tore families apart.

Marriage and Family

Isabella was working for the Dumont family in New York. She met Robert. He was a slave from a nearby farm. She loved him. Robert was caught visiting her. He was beaten by his owner and sent away. She never saw Robert again.

In 1814, Isabella agreed to marry Thomas. He also was a slave owned by the Dumonts. Slave owners liked slaves to marry and have children. Each child became a slave. In this way, owners increased their number of slaves.

Isabella and Thomas had five children. They were Diana, Elizabeth, Hannah, Peter, and Sophia.

Slaves were often beaten if they did not follow their owners' rules.

Free Woman

In 1817, New York passed a law that freed slaves. Owners had to set their slaves free within 10 years. Isabella's owner made her a promise. She could be free in nine years if she worked hard.

For nine years, Isabella worked long and hard. But her owner changed his mind. He refused to free her as he had promised. Isabella felt angry and cheated. She took her baby, Sophia, and ran away.

Isabella escaped to a nearby farm. Her owner found her. He wanted her back. The farmer and his family were against slavery. The farmer gave Dumont money to buy Isabella's freedom.

Isabella's owner promised to free her in nine years if she worked hard.

TO BE SOLD & LET

BY PUBLIC AUCTION,

On MONDAY the 18th of MAY, 1829,

UNDER THE TREES.

FOR SALE,

THE THREE FOLLOWING

SLAVES,

VIZ.

HANNIBAL, about 30 Years old, an excellent House Servant, of Good Character.

WILLIAM, about 35 Years old, a Labourer.

NANCY, an excellent House Servant and Nurse.

The MEN belonging to "LEECH'S" Estate, and the WOMAN to Mrs. D. SMIT

TO BE LET,

On the usual conditions of the Hirer finding them in Food, Clothes and Medical

MALE and FEMALE

SLAVES,

AS GOOD CHARACTERS,

ROBERT BAGLEY, about 20 Years old, a good House Servant.

WILLIAM BAGLEY, about 18 Years old, a Labourer.

JOHN ARMS, about 16 Years old.

JACK ANTONIA, about 40 Years old, a Labourer.

PHILIP, an Excellent Fisherman.

HARRY, about 27 Years old, a good House Servant.

LUCY, a Young Woman of good Character, used to House Work and the Nursery.

ELIZA, an Excellent Washerwoman.

CLARA, an Excellent Washerwoman.

FANNY, about 14 Years old, House Servant.

SARAH, about 14 Years old, House Servant.

Also for Sale, at Eleven o'Clock,

Fine Rice, Gram, Paddy, Books, Muslins, Needles, Pins, Ribbons, &c. &c.

AT ONE O'CLOCK, THAT CELEBRATED ENGLISH HORSE

BLUCHER,

The Fight for Her Son's Freedom

In 1827, the Dumonts sold Isabella's five-year-old son. He went to an Alabama slave owner. The sale was against the law in New York.

Isabella needed to take action. Otherwise, she would never see her son again. She walked a long distance to see a lawyer. A lawyer is a person who speaks for someone in court. Isabella needed the lawyer's help.

On the day of the trial, she saw her son. He had been beaten. He was afraid of his owner. He pretended he did not know his mother.

The judge decided in Isabella's favor. She won her case and kept her son. She was the first African-American woman to win a lawsuit in the United States.

Isabella's five-year-old son was sold to an Alabama slave owner. Posters like this one often told about the slaves.

Trouble in New York

Isabella moved to New York City in 1829. She went to work as a servant. Her husband, Thomas, was now free, too. But Thomas and Isabella agreed to separate.

Isabella was not happy in New York. She said the rich rob the poor. Then, the poor rob each other.

Isabella joined a church group. She worked hard for them and gave them money. The leaders were dishonest. When one of them died, the others blamed her. They accused Isabella of poisoning him. Again, she hired a lawyer and went to court. This time she fought for her good name. She won the case and was awarded money.

Isabella fought for her good name and won.

New Name, New Life

When Isabella was 44, she wanted to travel and speak. She wanted to tell people about her love for God. She left New York City.

She planned to sojourn. She wanted to travel and see new places. She said her only master now was God. She believed that God was truth. She gave herself a new name. She was no longer Isabella. She was Sojourner Truth. Her new name fit her new life.

Sojourner Truth traveled thousands of miles or kilometers across many states. She spoke about God. She gave powerful speeches against slavery. She talked about the rights of women. People came to hear her speak. She spoke with common sense and dignity. Dignity means self-respect.

Isabella changed her name to Sojourner, which means to travel.

Famous Speech

In 1851, Sojourner attended a convention for women's rights. It took place in Akron, Ohio. One speaker said that women were weak. He believed women should not have rights.

Sojourner wore a gray dress, a shawl, and a turban. A turban is a long scarf worn on the head. She stood tall and strong in front of the crowd.

She said nobody ever helped her into carriages and over ditches. Then, she rolled up her sleeve. She showed the crowd her strong arm. She talked about planting and plowing fields. She told the crowd about her children sold as slaves. She declared that she was a strong woman. Later, people called this her "Ain't I a Woman" speech.

Sojourner spoke about women's rights.

Book of Life

Sojourner Truth told her life story in a book. It was called *The Narrative of Sojourner Truth.* She earned some money from the book sales. She bought a house in Battle Creek, Michigan. She spent time there with her children and grandchildren.

Sojourner always carried a journal with her. She kept newspaper clippings, letters, and signatures of people she met. President Abraham Lincoln even signed her book. This signature was important to her. He was the president who signed the written order that freed slaves.

Sojourner Truth died on November 26, 1883, in Battle Creek, Michigan. She was 84 years old.

Sojourner Truth told her life story in the book *The Narrative of Sojourner Truth.*

Words from Sojourner Truth

"Man is so selfish that he has got women's rights and his own, too, and yet he won't give women their rights. He keeps them to himself."

From a speech to the Conference of American Equal Rights Association, New York City, 1867.

"If the first woman God ever made was strong enough to turn the world upside down all alone, these women together ought to be able to turn it back and get it right-side up again."

From a speech about women's right to vote given at the 1851 Women's Rights Convention in Akron, Ohio.

Important Dates in Sojourner Truth's Life

1797—Born in Hurley, New York

1806—Sold to John Neely

1808—Sold to Martin Schryver

1810—Sold to John Dumont

1814—Marries Thomas, a Dumont slave

1827—Freed from slavery

1828—Moves to New York City

1843—Changes name to Sojourner Truth and travels

1850—Publishes *The Narrative of Sojourner Truth*

1851—Gives the "Ain't I a Woman" speech in Akron, Ohio

1856—Moves to Battle Creek, Michigan

1864—Meets with President Abraham Lincoln

1878—Republishes *The Narrative of Sojourner Truth*

1883—Dies in Battle Creek, Michigan

Words to Know

dignity (DIG-ni-tee)—self-respect

lawyer (LAW-yur)—a person who speaks for someone in court

slave trader (SLAYV TRAY-dur)—a person who buys and sells slaves

sojourn (SO-gern)—to travel

turban (TUR-buhn)—a long scarf wrapped around the head

Read More

Claflin, Edward Beacher. *Sojourner Truth and the Struggle for Freedom.* New York: Barrons, 1987.

Oritz, Victoria. *Sojourner Truth: A Self-Made Woman.* New York: J.B. Lippencott Company, 1974.

Pauli, Hertha. *Her Name Was Sojourner Truth.* New York: Appleton-Century Crofts, 1962.

Shumate, Jane. *Sojourner Truth and the Voice of Freedom.* Brookfield, Conn.: Millbrook Press, 1991.

Useful Addresses

Detroit Historical Museum
5401 Woodward Street
Detroit, MI 48202

State University of New York
College at New Paltz
Sojourner Truth Library
New Paltz, NY 12561

Internet Sites

Sojourner Truth
http://www.ai.mit.edu/people/ellens/DP/truth.html
African-American History: Sojourner Truth
http://gopher.lib.virginia.edu/exhibits/rec_acq/history/truth.html

Index